First Love

Prayers

Prayers that Lead You into the Arms of God

-prayer book & journal-

Bethany Frazer

WestBow
PRESS
A DIVISION OF THOMAS NELSON

WestBow Press books may be ordered through booksellers or by contacting:

WestBow Press
A Division of Thomas Nelson
1663 Liberty Drive
Bloomington, IN 47403
www.westbowpress.com
1-(866) 928-1240

ISBN: 978-1-4497-0688-3 (sc)
ISBN: 978-1-4497-0689-0 (dj)
ISBN: 978-1-4497-0687-6 (e)
Library of Congress Control Number: 2010940434
Printed in the United States of America

WestBow Press rev. date: 3/24/2011

To Andrew:

My husband, you have been my inspiration
to continue,
to keep delving inside to find the gold hidden deep within.
You have been my greatest friend,
and
I will always love you!

Acknowledgements

What an amazing journey God is taking me on! I am *so grateful* for His help with this book. His leading and direction have been a constant. His love has been saturating. Thank you, Lord, for speaking to me *so clearly* how very deeply You LOVE us all! I love You too.

To Andrew: Thank you! You have successfully made me feel your love for me these past 10 years! This book needed your touch. Thank you for giving it and for being a living example of how much He loves me. I love you so very much.

To my 3: You have been amazing, patient and encouraging! Always remember your heavenly Father wants to know everything you are thinking. He is your "forever friend." I love you…1, 2 and 3.

To my family and friends (all of you!): What an amazing group! I have felt so much support from you all! And I want to say thank you for the encouraging texts, the generous words, and all of the ways each of you lets me know how much you care. You truly have made me feel so special. I love you!

Forward

Prayers put wings to our burdens. They eliminate the aches of the wounded heart. Praying is our pipe-line to God's peace. It is the anchor of our wavering soul. Bethany Frazer has given us a roadmap to God's heart; a train on which we can ride into the presence of God.

Bethany has in her book "First Love Prayers" given us a secret key into the heart of God. With each prayer you will feel your soul take flight, your spirit filled with the inspirational words of love & intimacy with God. No one can deny the blessing of fellowship with God. Have your stress relieved and your fear destroyed by the beautifully written words of this gifted writer.

Take time with each prayer. Use them as antibiotics for the ailments of the mind. Let them train your soul to pray Intimately. To treat God with faith and respect. "First Love Prayers" will change your way of conversing with God; helping make God tangible to you. Prepare yourself for the unveiling of God's face.

Prayers tell God we trust Him and believe He hears us. Soul prayers tell God we want Him and long for His abiding presence. Eat this feast of prayers and let your soul fly into God's arms.

-Ivan Tait (Founder of What Matters Ministries and Missions, Worldwide Evangelist, Missionary and Orphan Rescuer)
www.WhatMattersMM.org

Table of Contents

(Prayers listed by meaning)
Bolded numbers are recommended
if you have limited time ☺

The Lord As:

The Lord As continued...

The Guide / Shepherd
4, 14, 15, 16, 17, 18, 19, 20, 21, 22, 23, 24, 25, 27, 30,
34, 36, 40, 41, 43, 44, 47, 48, 49, 51, 52

The Healer
2, 13, 15, 18, 20, 22, 28, 50, 51, 52

Light
11, 12, 13, 14, 15, 16, 18, 19, 20, 22, 24, 25, 27, 28, 29,
30, 31, 36, 41, 47, 48, 49, 50, 52

Love
1, 12, 13, 14, 15, 16, 17, 18 ,19 , 20, 22, 23, 24, 27, 28,
29, 30, 32, 33, 35, 36, 37, 41, 42, 43, 44, 45, 46, 48,
49, 52

The Provider / The Planner
12, 13, 15, 16, 18, 20, 21, 22, 23, 26, 27, 29, 30, 31, 34,
38, 48, 49, 50, 51, 52

Your Teacher
4, 7, 13, 15, 16, 18, 20, 21, 22, 24, 26, 27, 28, 29, 31, 33,
34, 37, 39, 43, 44, 47, 48, 49, 52

Faithful
20, 24, 27, 28, 29, 30, 31, 34, 37, 39, 40, 41, 42, 47, 48,
49, 50, 51, 52

Your Creator
4, 16, 17, 37, 48, 52

The King of Kings
44, 48, 50

When You Need:

Strength
5, 11, 14, 15, 16, 18, 21, 22, 23, 24, 26, 29, 32, 39, 41, 48, 49

Encouragement
3, 4, 5, 8, 10, 11, 12, 14, 15, 16, 18, 20, 21, 22, 23, 25, 26, 27, 30, 31, 33, 34, 36, 38, 41, 43, 46, 48, 49

An Adventure
4, 7, 16, 17, 19, 20, 21, 22, 24, 26, 27, 29, 30, 33, 34, 37, 40, 41, 43, 49, 51, 52

Contentment
1, 14, 18, 19, 27, 31

Love
1, 4, 13, 14, 15, 17, 18, 19, 20, 22, 23, 30, 31, 32, 33, 37, 38, 39, 40, 41, 42, 43, 45, 49

Renewing
2, 8, 9, 10, 13, 15, 16, 17, 19, 21, 22, 23, 36, 37, 39, 41, 45, 49, 50, 52

His Presence / His Voice
1—52

Restoration / Wholeness / To Be Cleansed
1, 2, 5, 9, 10, 11, 12, 13, 14, 16, 17, 18, 19, 20, 23, 24, 25, 32, 37, 45, 46, 47, 48, 49, 50, 52

To Dream / Inspiration / Vision
5, 6, 7, 14, 16, 17, 19, 20, 21, 22, 24, 26, 27, 33, 36, 37, 41, 44, 45, 48, 49, 52

When You Need continued...

To Repent or Expose Something with Him
    1, 9, 11, 12, 13, 17, 18, 21, 24, 26, 32, 41, 45, 46, 48,
    50, 52

A New Self-Image
    1, 9, 10, 11, 13, 14, 17, 18, 21, 22, 23, 24, 25, 26, 27, 33,
    39, 41, 45, 49, 52

To Change
    1, 9, 10, 11, 13, 15, 18, 20, 21, 22, 24, 25, 26, 33, 35, 41,
    43, 47, 48, 49, 50, 52

To Be Close to Him
    1, 9, 10, 11, 12, 14, 15, 16, 17, 18, 19, 20, 21, 23, 24, 25, 26,
    27, 28, 29, 30, 33, 35, 36, 39, 41, 42, 44, 45, 47, 49, 52

To Overcome
    1, 10, 11, 12, 13, 15, 16, 17, 18, 20, 21, 22, 24, 26, 27,
    36, 40, 41, 50

Purpose for Yourself and For Life
    1, 9, 10, 13, 12, 15, 16, 17, 18, 19, 20, 21, 22, 23, 24, 25,
    26, 27, 28, 29, 30, 33, 34, 37, 39, 40, 41, 42, 50, 52

Wisdom
    1, 12, 13, 14, 15, 16, 17, 18, 20, 21, 22, 23, 24, 25, 26,
    34, 37, 41, 46, 48, 49, 50, 52

Understanding for Life & Self
    1, 3, 10, 11, 13, 15, 16, 18, 20, 21, 24, 25, 26, 27, 29, 30,
    32, 34, 41, 42, 46, 49, 50, 52

True Life
    1, 9, 10, 12, 13, 14, 15, 16, 17, 18, 20, 21, 22, 24, 26, 27,
    30, 36, 37, 38, 42, 45, 46, 49, 52

When You Need continued...

To Feel Safe & Secure
1, 10, 12, 14, 15, 16, 18, 20, 22, 23, 24, 26, 27, 30, 32, 33, 38, 41, 45, 46, 47

Forgiveness/Another Chance
1, 3, 10, 11, 12, 13, 15, 17, 18, 21, 22, 23, 24, 32, 37, 41, 46, 50, 52

New Revelation
1, 3, 7, 9, 10, 11, 12, 13, 14, 15, 16, 17, 18, 19, 20, 21, 22, 23, 24, 26, 27, 29, 36, 37, 41, 42, 43, 44, 49, 52

Growth
1, 3, 9, 10, 11, 13, 15, 17, 18, 20, 21, 22, 23, 24, 26, 27, 42, 45, 46, 48, 50, 52

Peace
9, 11, 12, 14, 15, 16, 17, 18, 19, 20, 21, 22, 23, 24, 27, 28, 29, 30, 32, 36, 39, 40, 41, 42, 45, 46, 48, 49, 52

To Know He's There & That He Cares
1—52

Hope
1, 3, 6, 8, 11, 13, 14, 15, 18, 19, 20, 21, 22, 23, 24, 26, 27, 28, 32, 33, 34, 36, 37, 38, 39, 40, 43, 44, 45, 46, 47, 48, 49, 50

His Mercy
9, 11, 13, 14, 15, 16, 17, 18, 19, 20, 21, 24, 30, 37, 41, 42, 43, 45, 46, 50, 51, 52

His Faithfulness
8, 11, 12, 13, 14, 15, 16, 17, 19, 20, 21, 22, 23, 24, 25, 27, 30, 31, 32, 34, 35, 36, 39, 41, 42, 45, 46, 48, 49, 50, 51, 52

When You Need continued...

When You Feel:

When You Feel continued...

<u>Alone / Lonely</u>
41, 42, 43, 47

<u>Incomplete</u>
1, 2, 11, 13, 14, 15, 16, 17, 20, 21, 22, 23, 24, 25, 26, 27, 28, 32, 35, 39, 42, 43, 45, 51

<u>Thankful</u>
1, 5, 11, 16, 17, 19, 20, 21, 22, 23, 24, 25, 27, 28, 29, 30, 31, 32, 33, 37, 38, 39, 40, 41, 42, 43, 44, 45, 49, 50, 51, 52

<u>Burdened</u>
11, 15, 16, 17, 18, 21, 22, 23, 24, 25, 29, 32, 36, 49, 50, 52

<u>You Desire Him</u>
1, 5, 6, 11, 12, 13, 14, 17, 19, 21, 22, 23, 24, 28, 30, 33, 35, 36, 39, 42, 43, 44, 49

<u>Like Worshipping & Praising Him / Love from or for Him</u>
2, 6, 12, 13, 14, 16, 17, 18, 19, 20, 21, 22, 23, 26, 27, 28, 30, 31, 32, 34, 35, 37, 39, 40, 43, 44, 45, 49, 50, 51, 52

<u>Humbled by His Love</u>
2, 9, 12, 14, 15, 16, 17, 20, 22, 23, 24, 28, 30, 31, 32, 37, 39, 40, 42, 43, 44, 45, 48, 49, 50, 51

<u>Like Giving Up</u>
14, 15, 20, 21, 22, 23, 24, 25, 32, 39, 41, 42

<u>Challenged / Convicted</u>
46, 50

Preface

The first title for this book was called "My Prayer to My Love." It has always been a book from me to God and from Him back to me.

It was 1999, I was away at Bible college in Sydney, Australia, and God started giving me beautiful prayers and asking me to write them down and re-read them over to myself after I was done. When I reread the prayers, I wept every time. He was expressing to me, through my own writing, how much He loved me—so much!

It was then He started leading me to put the prayers together in a book and share them with others. I gave them to only a handful of people and watched as God started blessing their prayer lives. I realized that the prayers He was giving me were not solely for my benefit, growth and encouragement, but were meant for far more than just me.

I feel honored that I am now able, 10 years later, to share these prayers with you. My hope is that they minister to you during different seasons of your walk and relationship with Him and that they help you grow closer and more intimate with Him as you seek Him and His presence for every facet of your life. **He really does love you—so much!**

A Note from the Author's Desk

To every one of you who are reading this book:
Open yourself up!
Desire the presence of God with each page you
turn, and let yourself be met there.
Be saturated in the love of the One who loved
you first.
Be enveloped in His arms and strengthened by
His words.
Draw from His person and drink of His strength.
Let Him love on you,
and learn how to love Him in return.

Psalm 23

You, LORD, are my shepherd. I will never be
in need.
You let me rest in fields of green grass. You
lead me to streams of peaceful water,
and you refresh my life. You are true to your
name, and you lead me along the right paths.
I may walk through valleys as dark as death, but
I won't be afraid. You are with me, and your
shepherd's rod makes me feel safe. You treat me
to a feast, while my enemies watch. You honor
me as your guest, and you fill my cup until
it overflows.
Your kindness and love will always be
with me each day of my life, and I will
live forever in your house, Lord.
(CEV)

Proverbs 15:8

God can't stand pious poses,
but he delights in genuine prayers.
(The Message)

Psalm 141:2

Let my prayer be set forth as incense before
You, the lifting up of my hands as
the evening sacrifice.
(AMP)

Psalm 141:2

God, come close. Come quickly! Open
your ears-it's my voice you're hearing!
Treat my prayer as sweet incense rising;
My raised hands are my evening prayers.
(The Message)

1

Oh Lord, You satisfy my soul.
Nothing is complete without You in it.
All I long for is to be near You.
I find my wholeness in Your arms.
In Your eyes I find satisfaction.

Excellence belongs to You,
And only in You can I find it.

From deep within I cry out for
Your touch;
I long to be in Your arms.
I come before You as though lost
and barren, yet You fill me.
You create life in my innermost being.
Safety and Security are free gifts
You give to me.
My insecurity vanishes with one look from Your eyes,
one touch from Your hand.

My soul finds rest in You.
My soul is calmed and quieted
within me,
For you long to satisfy
my every last desire.
Your will be fulfilled in my life.
I yearn to serve You.

Give to Your love a new heart.
Purify my mind; cleanse me from within.
I give You all of myself in exchange for
all of You,
For only in You do I find my *self*.
My desire is for You, My Love.

Notes & Your Personal Prayers to God

_____

_____

_____

_____

_____

_____

_____

_____

_____

_____

_____

_____

_____

_____

_____

_____

_____

_____

_____

2

Take me with You on Your journey.
Hold my hand.
I am misdirected and misled with all others but You.

I cannot live without Your breath
inside of me.
Your passion overwhelms me.
The words from Your mouth make
me shudder from within;
For You reach inside of me and touch every last part,
making everything whole.

I long to give of myself to You.
Love drives me to sacrifice all for You.
It drives me to serve You.
Please take heed and hear my words of love that I cry
from my soul within.
Your image is perfect.
All I need I see in You.
And without You I am incomplete.

First Love Prayers

I do not deserve such compassion,
such honor and glory
that You place on my head.
For without You I am nothing, and
with You I am all things.

You fulfill my soul,
And I long to love You
with every last part.

Notes & Your Personal Prayers to God

3

He cares for me.
He shows me love at no cost.
He opens Himself to me with
no reservation.
I hurt Him, I cut Him; He never leaves.
When I am faithless, He is faithful.
When I am abashed and ashamed,
He praises me, loves me, forgives me.
I never can be cast away,
cast aside for my failures.
With Him there is always another
open door, another chance,
Something always far above
my expectations.
My God is unfailing.
He is merciful, loving,
careful always of my feelings—
Always watching out for me.

No matter what I do,
He is always there.
And He always cares.

Lamentations 3:22–23

Through the LORD's mercies we are
not consumed,
Because His compassions fail not.
They are new every morning;
Great *is* Your faithfulness.
(NKJV)

Notes & Your Personal Prayers to God

4

He delights in me.
He opens His arms to hold me, squeeze
me, hear all my wild tales
and imaginings;
To listen closely to all my desires
and all my dreams,
The adventures I want to go on,
The people I want to meet.

He listens intently,
Nodding and jotting down every word,
Always making me feel like
I'm His favorite.
Like I matter more to Him than
anything else in the world.
So, therefore, I get His full attention
Because He loves me and takes joy
in everything we talk about.
Then, I realize how much I've been
talking—all about me.

First Love Prayers

I stop and I listen, and He talks to me.
He talks about me
Because He loves me;
He has plans for me.
Big dreams, big adventures.
Wild, impossible, unimaginable things
that amaze and shock me,
that blow me out of the water.

To believe the plans He has in store
for me,
And to believe how much time He
spends thinking about me.
How can I doubt how much He
loves me?

Notes & Your Personal Prayers to God

5

How can I say thank you for all
You've done for me?
How can I express what I feel inside?
My heart desires to show You my love;
To express to You my gratitude for
life, for love, for family,
For the air we breathe,
For the blessings You give.

There is nothing we can take pleasure in
that does not originate with You.

For You are Joy itself,
You are the essence of Love;
You are the Purity of life;
You are Who I long to be like.

To never be worried by trivial things;
To always care and have compassion
for those who've done me wrong.

To always see the beauty
in every single person.
To be strong and brave
in the face of adversity.
To believe in something *so much* that
I would give my life for it.

How could I say thank you for who
You are?
How can I express the gratitude
I have inside?
I love You;
I want to always be near You.
I want to always be close to You,
And to say thank you from the bottom of my heart.

Notes & Your Personal Prayers to God

6

You've got so many attributes
that I admire.
So many beauties in Your character.
So much passion in everything You do.
I love Your creativity
and Your ever-increasing imagination.
I love the talks we have of things to come
as we dream of our future together.

I never knew how wonderful life
could be;
How much I could dream
and hope and believe
in something I could not even see.

But when I'm with You it's so easy;
It's like two huge doors open before me when we talk.
Like huge barriers that would have been way too heavy

For me to open alone.
But with You they swing open lightly,
Almost excitedly, anticipating
our entrance.
And when we step inside there is a
world of dreams *in me* that arise,
and all at once seem possible.
It's amazing the way I feel when I spend time with You.
It's amazing how much You love me.

Notes & Your Personal Prayers to God

7

I peek into the room,
The hidden chamber of Your revelation.
We've been talking.
Sharing.
Expressing how we feel for one another,
And You've shown me new things.

You've opened doors inside of my
soul I never knew existed,
And You're taking me on a journey
into the hidden things of Your kingdom.
I am honored by Your trust in me.

You speak to me.
I am overwhelmed by all You've
prepared ahead of time.
All You've set in place.
The unbelievable way You love me.

How can I cherish what You've
shown me?
I never want to forget these feelings,
this revelation.
Obedience. Love. Prayer.
Fellowship. Sacrifice.

All I need to do is what You did on earth.
All I need to do is follow Your example.
All I need is You.

Notes & Your Personal Prayers to God

8

Your faithfulness astounds me.
I come to You yearning for You to
speak to me.
To say my name; to remind me and
confirm in me Your promises.
How I long for Your presence in a dry and thirsty land
where there is no water.
You are water.
You are my Savior.
You come down and meet me,
and touch me and fill me to overflowing.

Oh, how faithful You are.
Never ending, never changing, constant and forever.
Always mine and forever near me.
Yearning to speak with me and encourage me,
And show me the hidden places of
Your Spirit.
How I long to see them,
To enter into the Holy of Holies
And bask in Your presence—
Completely enveloped in Your love.

Notes & Your Personal Prayers to God

9

Search me, Lord.
Go within—deep within.
Root out everything
that does not bear Your mark,
That doesn't smell of Your perfume.
I want nothing that doesn't resemble Your face;
Nothing cracked or broken.
Beauty adorns Your works.
Holiness is seen in all Your creation.
Replenish the dryness of my soul.
Water it with Your salvation.
With Your mercy see my faults and
wash me clean.
I want all I am to smell of incense
that cries out Your name.

Holy, merciful, gracious God in
whom my soul takes its refuge,
You, Oh Lord, are my heart's desire.

Come into my heart and see me for
what I am.
In Your eyes I am beautiful;
In Your arms I am completed;
In Your mind I am caring.
Oh, how I yearn to be all
that You see me as.
But, only in You can all come to pass.
I want You to look inside of my life
and see Yourself, Lord.
I long to live my life as a reflection of Your grace,
Your beauty.

Notes & Your Personal Prayers to God

10

You always bless me with Your words.
Not one negative thought do You have toward me.
You long to see me prosper,
To see me reach wholeness
and completeness.

You thrive on my development,
For I am part of You.
I am made in Your likeness;
May I ever please You.

My desire is to make You smile,
To bring joy to Your heart.
I flourish in Your presence.

As Your child I know You care for me.
I see in Your eyes an acceptance
that can never be taken away,
no matter my failures.

First Love Prayers

Each and every day You add
new life to me.
You increase me more and more
Because there is nothing evil in You.

You long to see me conquer my fears,
To see me reach my purpose in You.
Your love sets a blanket of protection over my head,
And nothing can touch me.
You disarm the snare before I reach it
so that nothing can hinder me from coming to You.

Hold me in Your arms.
Sit me on Your lap.

Only with You am I safe.
Only there do I long to dwell.

Psalm 139:17-18

How precious also are Your thoughts to me, O God!
How great is the sum of them!
If I should count them, they would be
more in number than the sand;
When I awake, I am still with You.
(NKJV)

Notes & Your Personal Prayers to God

11

My soul melts as I smell Your
sweet fragrance.

The scent of oil on Your robe is heavy
in the air
and entices me into Your throne room.
I approach You heavy with my sin,
but longing to be made white as snow.
I cannot run from Your presence, nor long to,
For You have enlarged my heart
and strengthened my being
Just with one Word from Your mouth,
From one smell of Your glory.

I fall on my face.
I cling to Your garments.
I feel revived now.
I feel as though my help has finally come.
My distress is over; my burdens are
lifted and vanished forever.

First Love Prayers

Your truth opens my eyes.
You reach down and pick me up
out of my sorrow.
You have set me before men as a king.

Despite my failings, You see my future.
Your vision is not clouded by
my unworthiness.
The best is Your desire for me and

The best *I shall always be* in Your eyes.

Notes & Your Personal Prayers to God

12

Dwelling in Your courts I find
complete peace.
Lying at Your feet I find my restoration.

Prostrate before You, Lord, I come.
Kneeling at Your throne, I weep for joy.

Peace I have found in Your gaze.
Suffering has ended.
Gnashing of teeth shall be no more.

For in Your house there is safety;
in Your presence fullness of joy.

My struggle has ended and comfort
is now my portion—forever.

Worshipping You is all I desire.
In praising You,
my prayers are answered.

First Love Prayers

In seeking You is my destiny made clear.
For You alone hold the key to
my deepest wish.
My deepest yearning.
What I long for above all else—to be
near You.

To be enveloped in Your majesty.
To die to myself daily
So that I can see Your face more clearly.

To be Yours and dwell with You is what I live for.
You are my portion.

Psalm 16:11

You will show me the path of life; in Your
presence is fullness of joy, at Your right
hand there are pleasures forevermore.
(AMP)

Notes & Your Personal Prayers to God

13

In Your presence, Oh God, I long to be.
Take me, use me, develop me, Oh Lord on High.
Hide me in the secret place of
Your presence
Where the desires of Your heart become mine as well.

Please reveal Yourself to me;
I need You.
I cannot survive without You.
Make me one with Your purpose;
With Your plan make me knowledgeable,
That I may ever serve You.

Nothing I do has meaning unless *You* are by my side,
unless I do it for You,
because You are my satisfaction.
I am thirsty to drink of Your purpose.
Your mercy endures forever.
Open my eyes that I may see.
Remove all contempt from my soul;
Shed Your light on all the dark.

Weed out my soul.
Weed all self from my desires.
I only want You, Lord.
I only need You, my Love.
I want to breathe You in daily.
Refresh my being and give me new life.
Wholeness is found in You.

Psalm 27:5

For in the day of trouble He will hide me in His
shelter; in the secret place of His tent will He
hide me; He will set me high upon a rock.
(AMP)

Notes & Your Personal Prayers to God

14

I love when You invade my life,
my schedule, my routine.
I love the rush I feel when I'm busy
doing my thing,
and all of a sudden a wave of
incredible love washes over me.

I know right then that I'm faced with
the choice
Of continuing what I was doing,
Or dropping everything to be with You.

And when I let myself be enveloped by Your love,
Those times of communion where we talk, laugh, cry,
And share each other's hearts mean
so much to me.

Those moments are the ones that
keep me going when I feel like
Quitting in differing areas in life.
These are the moments I hold onto
and cherish,
And they always seem to hit me
by surprise—
And when I need them the most!

You are always amazing me with
Your tenderness
and how much You truly love me
and desire time with me.
Just us—together.

I love You!
And I am so thankful for this joy
of feeling so strongly...

Your love for me.

Thank you, *my Love.*

Notes & Your Personal Prayers to God

15

Thank you, Lord, for Your faithfulness.
When I am feeling weak or discouraged, You are there.
You pick me up.
You help me overcome.

I know that faith without works is dead—is nothing.
Therefore, *Your faithfulness to me* means
That *You are working things out for me!*
Working things together for my good!

Thank you, Lord!
No situation is too hopeless.
No situation is too overwhelming.
You are Faithful!
You are working things out for me.
Your thoughts toward me are higher
than I can even imagine.
You are with me,
You are Faithful!

Psalm 36:5

Your mercy and loving-kindness, O Lord, extend
to the skies, and Your faithfulness to the clouds.
(AMP)

Notes & Your Personal Prayers to God

16

Thank you, Lord!
Your blessings are from
everlasting to everlasting.
My soul bursts with the desire to
thank You
For all that You have done in my life.
To show You the deep gratitude
I have inside
For all of Your many blessings.
To pour out my soul within me in
total adoration of Your name.
I am eternally grateful,
and immeasurably
In love with You
for who You are to me.

You fill me to overflowing with the immense scope
Of destiny that You have laid out for me;
The plans You have made for my life.
Plans that surpass even my
wildest dreams
And encompass all of my deepest wishes.
All of my desires are met in You!

You have not left me lonely or lacking
any of the rich blessings
In the world You have created.
You leave nothing out, nothing missing.
You see my need and fill it, *as simple
and as complex* as that.
You bless me.

Whatever the need, whatever the desire.
You meet me where I'm at, and in
less than seconds,
You ease the load I'd been carrying
for so long.
Oh Lord, that I would learn to
seek You sooner,
Learning to trust and rely on You for
all things.
How my soul longs to know You deeper;
Thank you.

Psalm 145:16

You open Your hand
And satisfy the desire of every living thing.
(NKJV)

First Love Prayers

Notes & Your Personal Prayers to God

17

Your touch always astounds me.
I am brought to my knees and brought to tears because
Of Your great love.
With the hand that formed the earth,
With the hand that bled for my salvation,
You reached for me,
Longing for Your love to come home.
Never taking Your eyes from mine,
Never distracted from Your purpose.
To touch me,
To reach me
Is all that You desire.
To meet me where I am at so I can hear Your voice.

Gracious Father in heaven,
You consume me.
A warmth comes over me
as You approach.

I check my soul; I search my heart to see
if there is anything unclean or unworthy
to be seen by Your precious face,
and there is.
I want to run,
To hide because of my sin.
But I am made to stand still by
Your overwhelming gaze.

I am frightened to disappoint.
I try to keep You distant
By not running after You.
*Not pressing forward and seeking
Your face as You seek mine.*
I linger here and there,
My purpose, my destiny unclear.

Yet You, Lord, are never distracted;
Your vision never impaired.
And You reach me where I am at,
And You touch me.
I see Your face, and I receive revelation.

Praise be to the Lord
For never giving up,
For never turning away,
For *always* seeing my faults and
loving me still.

John 3:16

For God so greatly loved and dearly prized the world
that He [even] gave up His only begotten (unique)
Son, so that whoever believes in (trusts in, clings to,
relies on) Him shall not perish (come to destruction,
be lost) but have eternal (everlasting) life.

(AMP)

Notes & Your Personal Prayers to God

18

Torture and torment have seemed
my two greatest allies,
Despair and disdain my closest friends.
The noise of the waters has
filled my senses and
My eyes cannot see for the darkness
that seems to surround me.

Yet...*I close my eyes and then I learn to see.*
Hands lifted and heart opened, I see You.
Your light moves toward me in
the darkness.

Immediately, the night is quenched.
A new day breaks forth with the light.

I am afraid to open my eyes for fear
that the emptiness will return.
Then I see Your smile,
And my lack is filled.

Fear and fright vanish,
Leaving no memory left to linger.
How I need You in my life, Lord,
To quench the devices of the wicked one,
To be my Light and my Life.
All is in vain,
All is fleeting without *Your hand*
blessing it.

Relief and *release* have now comforted
my soul.
Peace and *purpose* are now the food for my thoughts.

Glory be to the Lord on High
For all of His mercy!
Let His kingdom reign forever;
His light never can be stifled!

Psalm 84:11

For the Lord God is a Sun and Shield; the Lord
bestows [present] grace and favor and [future] glory
(honor, splendor, and heavenly bliss)! No good thing
will He withhold from those who walk uprightly.

(AMP)

Notes & Your Personal Prayers to God

19

You spoke to me today—
Told me of my future, my destiny.

I love when You tell me things,
When You reveal to me things
yet to come.

How privileged I feel to know
You're thinking of me.
So honored to know I'm on Your mind.

Oh, how You love me;
I see it *and* I feel it.

Your love envelopes me and
brings me closer,
Drawing me nearer to You.

Oh, how *You love me,*
and *I love You...*
You are everything,
and I want to learn all there is to know about You.
I love You, *my* Lord!

Notes & Your Personal Prayers to God

20

I am so grateful.
I feel overwhelmed with gratitude for You, my Love.
You are so Faithful. So Present. So Real.

I see Your hand working for me.
Taking things and molding them,
Changing them *for me*.
You love me.
You desire closeness with me,
and for me to see Your face.
You're bringing me closer to You.

I'm keeping myself *open* to all You want to tell me.
I desire to learn from You!

Everything You hold for me is
precious, beautiful,
Wrought entirely for me

From Your love for me.
You care so much for me,
and You've planned so much for me.
I am grateful;
I am thankful for all You've done,
and all You are doing.
Thank you, Lord!

Thank you for loving me,
For giving so much for me with no
guarantee of any return
Except *Your faith* in me,
and *Your trust* in who I am—*who You
see me as.*

I love You, Lord!
Thank you!
I am *so* grateful.

Psalm 17:5

My steps have held closely to Your paths
[to the tracks of the One Who has gone
on before]; my feet have not slipped.
(AMP)

Notes & Your Personal Prayers to God

21

Oh Lord, help me to be faithful to
my calling.
To keep pressing on and keep enduring.
To run my race and finish well.
To finish—bringing honor to the King.

May the world know Whom I love.
May they always know Whom I serve.

Oh, how I love You, Lord!
I desire to fulfill my calling,
to accomplish my destiny *on time*.
Not to *fall behind* because of
my weaknesses,
my procrastinations.
I long to become all that I can be,
to develop all that is within me.

I know that You have placed inside
of me *treasures of gold;*
things that the world needs.
May I ever be mindful of Your call
on my life.

May I reach the end and hear these
beautiful words spoken over me:
"Well done, *My good* and *faithful servant.*"

Lord, I long to serve You
with all that I am.
Hear my cry;
Know my heart.

For *all* that I desire *is in You.*

Notes & Your Personal Prayers to God

22

Thank you, Lord, for this day!
Thank you, Father, for this
magnificent planet!
Thank you for the chance to live
another day!
My soul longs to magnify Your name
like creation does!

The mountains declare Your majesty.
The sea demonstrates Your strength.
The sun radiates Your splendor.
The seasons reflect Your wisdom.
The flowers display Your beauty.
The stars mesmerize all with
Your wonder.

I am at awe with Your creativity;
Your genius astounds me.
Oh, that I could be a part in creation
that magnifies Your name.

First Love Prayers

Let it be said of me:
that my feet trod the earth for
Your kingdom,
my hands healed the sick in Your name,
my eyes saw the needy and helped them,
my mouth spoke Your words to
the nations,
my heart followed earnestly after You.

This is what I desire—
To follow after You and
Bring glory to Your name in all that I do.

See: Genesis 1 (in The Amplified Bible)

Notes & Your Personal Prayers to God

23

Thank you for trusting me.
You always believe what I tell You.
You have faith in me,
That I will overcome.
You think so many good thoughts
toward me.
You are generous with Your love,
and with Your compliments to me.
You truly love me.
I can always trust that
You'll believe the best of my
heart's intentions.

You know me
Unlike anyone else ever could;
You're true.
The best friend anyone could ever
ask for.

You're truly loyal to me,
And You always *lift me up.*
Thank you for trusting me;
I will always trust You too.

Psalm 34:1

I will bless the Lord at all times;
His praise *shall* continually *be* in
my mouth.
(NKJV)

Notes & Your Personal Prayers to God

24

The depth of Your belief in me
inspires me to greatness.
I believe in myself because
You believe in me.
You are teaching me the meaning
of faithfulness.

Always believing and *always doing*—
moving forward.

You are guiding me,
Taking me on a grand adventure
with You.
Leading me where my heart longs
to explore.
We are uncovering treasures together;
I love this life.
I love Your Word.

The truth of Your Word brightens
the path in front of me,
A "How?" begins to form in my mind.
Questions start to arise:
"Where should I turn?"
"Where should I go?"
I am always assured of the answers
to come, for You are with me.

Always leading me;
Always guiding me.
A *constant* believer *in me.*

Notes & Your Personal Prayers to God

25

Direct my steps, Oh Lord.
Lead me in paths of righteousness.
Direct my compass,
Steer my course.
Align my paths,
That I may walk the straight and narrow.

Lead me down Your way,
For *You designed my course.*

You know the beginning and the end,
And You see the steps in between.

You visit with me.
You talk with me.
You show me the desired way.
You reveal to me Your plan.

Guide me, I pray,
That I may not veer off the path.
That I may not wander to-and-fro,
That all my steps will be favorable;
All my choices straight.
That I will aim well and hit the mark.

First Love Prayers

I do not wish to be mediocre for You.
To reside in the shadows, never sure of where to turn,

Too afraid to choose.
But rather: directed, led, steered onward
By a hand and a destiny too big for me
to withstand.

Lord, to be led by You,
This is my heart's desire.

Psalm 37:23-24

The steps of a *good* man are ordered by the LORD,
And He delights in his way.
Though he fall, he shall not be utterly cast down;
For the LORD upholds him with
His hand.
(NKJV)

Notes & Your Personal Prayers to God

26

Thirsty I come to You,
Hungry for the meat of Your Word—
For the revelations to build
my life upon,
The answers to change the world,
To save the lost and heal the sick.
The power to mend the wrongs done
to men,
The love to save the poor.
For the courage to live as You did.

How I desire strength in every fiber
of my being;
To influence the world for You.
To take charge, to take a risk, to take
a chance and come out on top.
To see a problem and solve it.

I desire, Lord, for You to use me;
To teach me the meanings in Your Word,
To show me the hidden things,
To learn directly from You, becoming more like You.

I long for faith that does not falter when life hits hard,
A revelation that does not bend to
the pressure of this world,
A conviction that's unchanging,
A love that's unconditional,
A heart that beats the very rhythm
of heaven,
A soul that sings the chorus of the angels,
And whose life and source is *only* You!

I love You, Lord!
And I desire to be used by You
With all that You have given me.

Teach me Your statutes,
Instruct me in Your ways, and
I shall listen;
I shall grow strong.

And one day I shall defeat an army
for my King!

2 Timothy 2:20-21

But in a great house there are not only vessels of
gold and silver, but also of wood and clay, some
for honor and some for dishonor. Therefore if
anyone cleanses himself from the latter, he will
be a vessel for honor, sanctified and useful for
the Master, prepared for every good work.
(NKJV)

Notes & Your Personal Prayers to God

27

You really do take care of everything.
You bring all of the pieces together
for me—
Things I never knew were meant to
be together.
And You show me the pattern.

You've been taking care of everything!
Taking care of me,
Working it all together,
Blessing me on every side;
I am so blessed by You, Lord!

I have nothing to fear,
Nothing to worry about,
For You are with me.

You lead me
And guide me,

And make known Yourself to me,

Woven throughout the fabric of my life.

You have always been with me—
And always will be.

Notes & Your Personal Prayers to God

28

How I long to drink of You more deeply,
To feel completely saturated in Your love,
To be overwhelmed by Your presence,
To bask in the glory of Your throne room,
To dream of one day touching You,
Of one day sitting beside You,
Of looking into Your eyes
and seeing me in them.

To finally understand what You must have felt for me,
To be able to give up *Your only*
Son because *You love me.*
To turn Your back on the One You love
For someone who didn't even know
Your name.
Someone who cannot live a day
now without Your touch,
Without Your voice,
Without Your presence in my world.

Oh, how I love Your voice.
My body rejoices at the sound of
Your name.
Lord, how I long to know You more,
Long to drink deeper of Your being,
And *see You* clearer than
ever before.

When You call me into Your
throne room,
into a secret place we share,
Where all my worries, fears and
doubts subside—
There is where I find peace;
Peace that lasts a lifetime.

Where I find my well,
A spring of living water that never
dries up,
Never vanishes.
Where I find You:
The Lover of my soul.

Psalm 27:4

One thing have I asked of the Lord, that will I
seek, inquire for, and [insistently] require: that
I may dwell in the house of the Lord [in His
presence] all the days of my life, to behold and
gaze upon the beauty [the sweet attractiveness
and the delightful loveliness] of the Lord and to
meditate, consider, and inquire in His temple.
(AMP)

Notes & Your Personal Prayers to God

29

When I feel overwhelmed, I come to You.
I come to You for peace,
For clarity, and understanding.
I seek You out for answers and for justice.
The feeling that everything is going to work out right;
Everything will be fine.

I start thanking You for my peace,
my answers,
and everything starts to get brighter.
The burdens start to be lifted,
Everything starts coming into focus.
The truth is revealed,
and I understand.

I see You there beside me;
You've been with me the whole time,
just waiting
For me to acknowledge and include You

So that You can do life with me.
So that You can illuminate the path before me,
Making a clear way for me
That I may run!
...as You expand my future in front
of me.

Thank you for always being with me!
Thank you for always being there
beside me,
Waiting for me to include You.
I love You.
Thank you!

Notes & Your Personal Prayers to God

30

Your hand guides me,
Leading me where I should go,
Taking me on this journey
that is my destiny.

Eagerly I listen to Your voice
Telling me where I should go.
All Your paths laid out for me,
Waiting for me to obey.

I am excited about my calling!
I am thrilled at my purpose!

That You laid this all out for
me—it astounds my mind!
So much more than I could ever
have imagined!

And I know that You're next to me...

Walking beside me,
Keeping me company,
Holding my hand.

First Love Prayers

Always my closest companion,
Always my friend.
We'll go on this journey together,
And I'll finally succeed!

Notes & Your Personal Prayers to God

31

All praise and all honor go to You, Lord!
All worship.
All glory.
You are worthy to be praised!

I feel total joy at how much love I receive from You.
I see You everywhere in my life, and
it is exciting!
You really do love and care for me.
You are so faithful to me.
Thank you for Your grace.

Although I am not perfect,
You never fail.
You are always there—
Always the same constant source
of my joy and happiness.
You fill me to overflowing.

I am so grateful for all You are to me.
All You do for me.
All You've shown me.
The light You've shed in my life.

Thank you.
Thank you for saving me!
Thank you for loving me first!
You are such a good God!

Notes & Your Personal Prayers to God

32

I search through Your Word for
some meaning,
Some answers to the question "Why?"
I see throughout it that You're holy,
That You're just,
That You're powerful.
My heart yearns to grasp the concept of
"Why" You made *me* for fellowship
with You.

I, who cannot give You anything
in return
For the life You've given me.

I am perplexed and amazed by Your wondrous love—
All of the sacrifices You've made for me,
All of the times I've failed, and
You've forgiven,

Times I choose other "things" instead
of You.

First Love Prayers

"Why" are You so good to me?
"Why" does my heart ache when I'm
not near You?
How can this be, though I've
never seen You?

Yet I have!
I've seen You in Your Word.
I've seen Your hand in my life.

Then I get the answer to the "Why?"
It is all because You love me!

And that love conquers everything!
That love can wade through any torrent,
withstand any trial;

That love has set me free...

To love another.

Psalm 25:14

The secret [of the sweet, satisfying companionship]
of the Lord have they who fear (revere and worship)
Him, and He will show them His covenant and
reveal to them its [deep, inner] meaning.

(AMP)

First Love Prayers

Notes & Your Personal Prayers to God

108

33

When I seek You, I love that I *know* I *will* find You.
It doesn't take very long—
Just a moment,
Just a second and I'm connected again
to You.
We're fellowshipping together.
You always have something to share
with me.
You love me *so* much,
And I can tell that You desire
my company.

I love spending time with You.
Talking with You brings such clarity to my life,
Such hope for the future,
Such expectation of good things
to come—
Of the desires of my heart
coming to pass.

You bless me so much with Your words.
The *thoughts* You think toward me
are amazing!
You are gracious and You are kind!

Thank you for loving me!
Thank you for being my friend!
I love You!

Notes & Your Personal Prayers to God

34

I trust You, Lord.
You are so faithful to me.
You have done *so many* good things for my life,
And I love how You care for me.
You carry my burdens, and You
give me answers.
You show me the Light, the Truth.
You answer my questions, and You
speak to me about my future.
Giving me hope and answers for things yet to come;
A direction for the days ahead.
I can trust in You.

You ready me for the future.
The things *You see* that I don't see yet.
The days still to come that You are preparing me for.
How wonderful to have You by my side,
On my team, helping prepare me for life.
I trust You, Lord!
You are so good to me.

Notes & Your Personal Prayers to God

35

I love You, Lord…
You are so amazing, Lord!
I don't want to box You in, Lord, with
different types of limitations.
I don't want to miss out on *any part*
of what You have for me,
due to weakness, neglect, or unfaithfulness.
You are AMAZING, God!

I love You…
I want everything You have!
Please don't hold back in my life, Lord;
Fill it to overflowing!
Mold and shape every aspect of
who I become,
of Your Spirit within me.
Place Your thumbprint on *every facet*
of my day.
I want Your plan to become the *reality*
of my life.

The "everyday" that makes up my
day to shout Your *majesty*,
Your *presence* saturating every part of it!

I love You...
I want EVERY part of You!
I want to soak up more than I
can contain.
To live in *Your glory* on a daily basis,
Reflecting Your face in my life.

Notes & Your Personal Prayers to God

36

All the thoughts consume me.
My mind swirling around like
a whirlpool,
trying to drag me under.
I want peace.
I want my mind to find its rest.

To *choose* my thoughts,
And have *time for dreaming*.

I want to talk with You with
no distraction,
To share my deepest wants, needs,
and desires
Without all of the shallow surface
issues in life
Trying to push their way to the top!

I feel as though my heart is yearning to be near You.
I want to share my deepest thoughts
with You,
But the mundane things of life
can take up all of my time.

So, I go to Your Word—
I read Your Word and my mind begins
to calm.
I see *everything* more clearly—and life gets brighter!

The world begins to take shape again;
The *daily things* in life begin to take
their rightful place again.
Everything begins to order itself,
And *I am at peace.*

Your presence surrounds me, and *I feel joy*—
Joy overwhelming!

Happiness:
that You are so near me,
That *I can feel You* all around me.

How precious You are to me, Oh Lord!
Thank you for Your Word;
Heavenly Father,
Thank you for Your peace!

Romans 12:2

Don't copy the behavior and customs of this world, but
let God transform you into a new person by changing
the way you think. Then you will learn to know God's
will for you, which is good and pleasing and perfect.

(NLT)

Notes & Your Personal Prayers to God

37

In Your *freedom* is where I want to live.

You are continually surprising me with Your hand
In every single part of the tapestry that makes my life.

You add such beautiful threads to me,
Laced with brilliant silvers and golds.

When I look back on my life, I
see such *grace* and *favor*.
You were always there adding
such beauty,
such *miraculous, astonishing*
elements to my everyday life.

You chose **me** from the beginning
of creation
To *lavish* Your love upon,
To fill my life with every good and
pleasant thing You have to offer.

There is *none* so generous, so good,
so faithful as You, Lord.
How can I say "thank you" enough?

I Love You, Lord…

Thank you for *all* that You've given
to me.
And for showing me throughout my life
how much You love ME!

Notes & Your Personal Prayers to God

38

I have *so much* to thank You for!
So many ways You've blessed my life.
So many places where I can see
Your hand at work—for me.

My life would not be the same.
My marriage, my children, my family;
Nothing stands alone apart from You.
You've touched every part of
who I am and what I have.

How can I say thank you?
Someone who holds the sun and
the moon in His hands—
Who's formed the earth and sky with
His words,
Whose mind no man can understand,
Who measures the span of the ocean
in a moment,
Who knows each hair when it falls
from my head.

But, *I am thankful,*
And *I am grateful*
For *all* You've done for *me!*

And inside I know that You know
How very much I love You!

Thank you...for everything!

Notes & Your Personal Prayers to God

39

Many times I come to a place of *desire*.
Not knowing how to express my
love for You,
My desire to be near You and to
know You more!

I wish I could express to You the way I feel for You
in words that would touch Your heart
so deeply
that You could truly feel my love.

Each and every time I start to feel
this desire for expression,
I start to remember how well
You know me.
How every time I am lonely, confused,
remorseful, distraught,
Nothing can soothe me like You do
Because You know me so well!

And I believe this connection we share
shows You how much I feel for You,
That *You do* feel that deep touch in Your heart when I
try to express my love to You.

And that You will never ever be in doubt
of *my* love for *You,*
my Lord.

Notes & Your Personal Prayers to God

40

He knows me so well—
Inside and out, and all around.

I sit here thinking— thinking of
everything and nothing all at once.
Wondering if I'm doing what I'm
meant to be doing right there
and then at that time in my life, my day.
Oh, You know me so well.
I feel You tugging at me,
Wanting me to spend more time
with You.
Drawing me into You.
And here I am floating on the outside,
uncommitted to Your call.

You know me so well…
I look as though I am on the outside
now, but how can I resist You?
You say the words that my soul can hear.

You reach out and touch me with Your
words, with Your direction.
I respond to Your voice, and Your direction comes.
A path set before me, awaiting my
first steps—
a journey to see You more,
of basking in Your presence.

All You wanted was to talk with me,
to be with me and fellowship together.
All You wanted was to say You love
me and want the best for me.
Not to worry or fret over anything,
For You are with me.
Always and forever.
To give me peace, that which I
was looking for all along.
Oh, You know me *so well*.

Thank you, God, for loving me!

Notes & Your Personal Prayers to God

41

I didn't feel close to You today.

I was drifting, feeling alone, lost.

I was going through my regular day with no vision,
No purpose to speak of.
To do my duty; do what is right.

I wanted You—
I needed to feel You there with me
to light the grey horizon.

How is it that I can live and not feel You?
Walk alone and not talk to You?
Breathe and not thank You?

Everything I am and everything I
have are all because of You.
Yet I don't always acknowledge
You in my everyday life.
I am my life, and I can act as though I am a sole island,
separate unto myself, doing what must be done today.

I separate myself from others, from
feeling all there is to feel,
And sometimes lose my touch to You.

Then I find a moment in my day,
my week, my year—
When I remember the reason
I'm alive,
The reason my heart is beating,
And it begins to race inside me.
I remember who You are and who I am; *why* I am.
I feel my love for You *begin to burn*
inside of me…dormant so long.

As I begin to think on my love for You, You
appear right beside me— Walking, talking,
smiling, speaking to me incredible truths,
Answering questions that I've kept hidden inside.
You understand all of my most
personal feelings,

And then in that instant I am there with You again…

And I am close to You.

Psalm 139:7-10

Where can I go from Your Spirit?
Or where can I flee from
Your presence?
If I ascend into heaven, *You are there;*
If I make my bed in hell, behold,
You are there.
If I take the wings of the morning,
And dwell in the uttermost parts of the sea,
Even there Your hand shall lead me,
And Your right hand shall hold me.
(NKJV)

Notes & Your Personal Prayers to God

42

The busyness of life consumed me today.
I was taken up in my work, in my chores.
I felt scattered and distant from any
true emotion.
I was floating through my day with
no real time
for anyone or anything.
All the "things" accomplished felt
like nothing
at the end of the day.

I have finished my day and I take my
first real moment
with You—and with myself.
And I ask myself, "How can I do
so much and feel so little?"
Purpose, Meaning—words that haunt me at night.
The desire to please You, to do Your
will in my everyday life.
To be close to You
While I'm working, reading, driving;
always to be near to You.

First Love Prayers

The day comes to an end,
And there in my bed You hold me
So close I feel enveloped.

Your arms encompassing me,
telling me *You were always there* with me.
So close You could smell the soap
on my hands as I cleaned,
So close You can see the ink stain on
my finger.
That You long *to be with me* as I long
to be with You,
that these moments we share together
are precious,
And that *You are pleased with me.*

Notes & Your Personal Prayers to God

43

I don't know where to start.
I open up Your Word, lost.

Where to begin?
What should I read?
Where do You want me to go?

I decide on the familiar,
Which I have already read and
know well.
Where many revelations have come to
me before,
And as I read, You lead me away.

You lead me *to Your death, and my life;*
To Your crucifixion.

And I see so many things You want to teach me:
Sacrifice, faithfulness, love.
Every area something I can work on;
Every topic challenging.

But You take me deeper.
There is more You want me to see,
More You need me to pick up
From Your pain and Your sacrifice.

You want me to see *You* better.
You are trying to reveal Yourself to
me more.
Not merely giving me principles to live by, but *You*—

Who You are.
How You feel and think.
Why You lived among us.
How You feel about me.
Why You did the things You did for
us on earth.
And I feel blessed.

Overwhelmed that You could truly want
me to know You better—
Your personality and what makes You pleased, happy,
what moves You.
I want to know more,
And I soak it up.
Every word, every feeling that You're showing me.

And I want more time with You.
More time like this to learn about You,
and to feel Your presence *all* around me.
I love You.

I have so much to learn about You.
Please continue to show me.

I desire to know all I can;
to feel all Your love for me.

Thank you!
For making it real in
showing me Yourself,
And for *never* giving up.

John 14:20-21

At that time [when that day comes] you will
know [for yourselves] that I am in My Father,
and you [are] in Me, and I [am] in you.
The person who has My commands and keeps
them is the one who [really] loves Me; and whoever
[really] loves Me will be loved by My Father,
and I [too] will love him and will show (reveal,
manifest) Myself to him. [I will let Myself be clearly
seen by him and make Myself real to him.]
(AMP)

Notes & Your Personal Prayers to God

44

You are magnificent, Lord!

Mighty and amazing are Your works!

Your throne room adorned with
jewels and precious stones.
Your kingdom wealthy beyond compare.
You are *so* beautiful!
Wow, You are my God,
My best friend.

You speak to my spirit;
You remind me of how much
You cherish me,
And *I stand amazed,*
In awe of Your grace on my life.
Those eyes, that face, Your smile;
To look upon Your face,
beholding Your beauty.

I cannot imagine anything
more spectacular.

One day we will walk together in the heavenly garden
You've grown for me.
Face-to-face, I'll gaze upon Your beauty and majesty.

What a day that will be!
A day to live for with *all* that I am!

On that day I desire to be presented
to You
with *all* the beauty of Your image,
Your face, shining out of me.

My life a reflection of Your beauty—
A jewel gleaming for You!

Notes & Your Personal Prayers to God

45

Oh, how much You love me, Lord.

I see Your hands of grace working
in my life.
I feel Your words healing the
broken pieces of my heart.

I know Your love—
So real.

I am with You,
And I feel overwhelmed by Your tenderness and
gentleness toward me.

You speak so kindly to me;
You love me *so* true.

So real—Your feelings for me.
They overwhelm all fear and confusion.
They wash over all self-critical doubts.

You restore and *make new.*
Your plans—nothing I could have
ever seen of my own imagining.

You love blessing me!
You want to bring me a harvest!

All of my dreams become a realization.
You love me more than I can ever know,
And that I know just from what I can see!

Notes & Your Personal Prayers to God

46

Is my heart truly sold out to You?
Do You own every part?
Do You know every area?

Is there any area I've kept hidden,
Unopened, unexposed to Your sight, Your eyes?

Who am I kidding to think I can hide
anything from You, God?
How foolish to imagine my faults are
not seen,
That life just goes on.
These areas left un-dealt with,
not affecting my destiny, my future.

But, *You love me too much!*
I see it *every day,*
You gave me the Helper—
You gave me the Holy Spirit.

He is my best friend.
He knows all,
Challenges me on all my faults,
Encourages me to take *all* things to You,
Teaches me how to live at a continual
state in Your presence.
He loves me, as You do.
He carries Your heart and Your thoughts.

He connects me to the right people.
How wonderful to have *so* many
cheering me on,
Rooting for *victories* in my life!
You truly have given me every way
to succeed.

Trust…
Trusting God with my whole life,
With my whole heart.
Opening up every part of my heart—
All I hold dear,
Every treasured memory—
To Your gaze.

Take *everything*, Lord!

I want everything that You have
for me, Lord.

Only You know the ending of my story,
And I want to reach "the end" with You at my side!

You are my prize;
Proof I ran the race, and ran it well.

Psalm 62:8

Trust in, lean on, rely on, and have confidence in
Him at all times, you people; pour out your hearts
before Him. God is a refuge for us (a fortress and a
high tower). Selah [pause, and calmly think of that]!
(AMP)

Notes & Your Personal Prayers to God

47

I tell You, "I trust You."
Do I really mean it?
Am I living those words?
Is my life a testimony of
living *faith in God*?

Does *my world* scream, "Jesus is here!";
That "God dwells in this place"?
This *is* what I want!
I desire to serve You!
I desire Your presence to be *near* me
at all times!

I long for closeness with You!
I want You here,
Now and *forever*!
You say, "I will *never leave* you,
nor forsake you!"
Your words bring comfort.
I start breathing easier now;
You will never leave me.

I will never feel lost, barren, alone,
Forgotten by the world and mankind.

Your presence begins soaking me with
joy and hope—*Everlasting.*

I will rest in You,
And You will keep me safe.
My Father and my God,
Almighty One!

Notes & Your Personal Prayers to God

48

Do I even act like I know You sometimes?
Does my life show Your glory?
Am I willing?
Am I obedient?
Do I sacrifice when asked for it?
Do I praise You even when my world looks bleak?
Am I a child worthy of the
title "Christian"?
Do I love You more than I love myself?
Am I *all* You have created me to be?
Am I making my soul known to You?
Are You familiar with the sound of
my prayers
making their way to heaven?
Am I pleasing You, Lord…my life a living example?
A life testimony pointing to the
One, True King?

There seem to be always *more areas for me to grow,*
But that is where You reside!

First Love Prayers

You take *all* of the questions
and doubts.
You are pleased when I talk to You,
Every time I meet with You.

You love me so much that it
does not matter
how many areas I still need to improve.
You are faithful still.

You remain ever present;
Loyal Friend through till the end.

You are always true to my calling and
my destiny.
Filling me with *new* hope,
And *ever-increasing new vision* into
my heart.
You fill until overflowing.

You are God.
You are Faithful!
You create everything I could ever need.
You created me.

You love that which You create;
That means, with all the improvements
I still need in my life,
You love me ALL the same!

I am so full of hope and dreams,
And every time I look into Your face,
I see a smile—directed back at me.
Thank you, Lord, for loving me:
Unconditionally.

Romans 8:39

No power in the sky above or in the earth
below—indeed, nothing in all creation will
ever be able to separate us from the love of God
that is revealed in Christ Jesus our Lord.
(NLT)

Notes & Your Personal Prayers to God

49

You make me new;
You fill my cup.
How I feel?
Overflowing.

Overflowing with abundant blessings and promise.
Immeasurable are Your gifts into my life.
Everywhere I look *I see Your blessing*
and favor.

Our relationship started with a *free* gift:
The greatest of all—Your Son.

You have shown me from
the very beginning
what Your character is like,
And how You will bless me and treat me.
I am sorry for doubting Your ability to provide for me.
In the seemingly rough times,
You were always there.

My belief and obedience swinging
wide the doors of blessing!
You have amazing plans for my life,
And I want to live in all the promise
that *Your* destiny creates in me!
Thank you, Lord!
Let it be done in my life, Lord. Amen.

Notes & Your Personal Prayers to God

50

Expose, Expose, Expose!
Take *everything* off!
I don't want any grotesque,
ugly infections
or diseases attaching themselves to
my destiny,
My calling, and my blessings.
Leeching resources from my harvest.
Remove *all* locusts from the fields.

Any hidden part I expose to Your light.
Clean the house!
Make every part new!
I choose You, God—
You and You alone!

This world's temptations hold *no* candle to the
mysteries of Your Word.

The wealth of this world has *no*
comparison and resembles not the
richness of Your kingdom.
Your will be lifted up!

You are light; You are life!
I give *all* I possess to You.

Wash me; make me clean.
Expose and purify every last part
So that nothing sickly can ever
live in me;
Nothing displeasing to You, Lord.
Nothing that reeks of this world's smell—
Its failing ideas and methodologies.

I want purity, cleanliness, truth;
To sow and then reap,

To be a light in this generation.

I want the Light and the Son, Who also is my Shield.

And I know with You I can have it.
All I need do is ask…

Psalm 84:11

For the Lord God is a Sun and Shield; the Lord
bestows [present] grace and favor and [future] glory
(honor, splendor, and heavenly bliss)! No good thing
will He withhold from those who walk uprightly.
(AMP)

𝒩otes & 𝒴our 𝒫ersonal 𝒫rayers to 𝒢od

51

I love You; I love You.
I love *You*, Lord.

There is none like You.

Thank you, Father, for Your love for me.
Thank you for caring for me,
for leading me and for healing me.

Thank you, Father, for Your faithfulness.
Thank you for Your tender mercies.

I love *You*, Lord…

I Love You, I Love You, I Love You.

There is none like You.

Thank you, Lord, for saving me.
Thank you, Father, for caring for
my family

And for *ALL* that concerns me!
I love You, Lord, and thank *You*
for all of these things—
For *You are worthy of all praise!*

Thank you, Lord. Amen.

Notes & Your Personal Prayers to God

52

...and I meet with You.
I turn all the lights off, and I sense
You're here.

Your Spirit overwhelms me, and I
stand speechless before You.
Humbled by Your love for me;
Your desire to be near me.

I listen; I feel You there, wooing me to come closer.
Wooing me to embrace You, as You have embraced me.
I let go;
I release all of my pride, all hurt,
all resentment and bitterness
That I've been holding for others and...for myself.

I run toward You, my arms open wide,
Heart racing just to touch You;
To feel as though we are one.

That for just this instant I can let it all go,
And that we can be together, away from it all.
That this moment can be ours—alone.

No one else intruding.
No one else speaking, interrupting
this beautiful silence we share.
And there in the dark of my room...

I meet with You.

Notes & Your Personal Prayers to God

Prayer for Salvation & Baptism in the Holy Spirit

"Heavenly Father, I realize that I am a sinner, and that I need salvation. I believe that Jesus died on the cross as payment for my sins, and that He rose again three days later and is living today (Rom. 10:9-10). I ask You, Jesus, to come into my heart and wash me clean from all my sin. I ask You to be Lord of my life. I receive You as my Lord and Savior. Thank you, Jesus, for saving me and forgiving me from all sin. I believe I am washed clean, have eternal life, and I am going to heaven when I die! In Jesus's name I pray, amen."

You are now a child of God, and this is the start of a brand new life and adventure with Him! God also promises that He will give the Holy Spirit to those who ask Him (Luke 11:13). The Holy Spirit is described in the Word as Your Helper, as well as the supernatural power in your life.

"Heavenly Father, I also ask You to fill me with the Holy Spirit—to be my Helper and give my life power to live for You. I fully expect to speak with other tongues as You give me utterance (Acts 2:4), in Jesus's name, amen!"

Now thank and praise God for filling you with the Holy Spirit! Start speaking out the words and syllables you receive—not in your own language but the language the Holy Spirit is giving to you. As you speak out the words and syllables you feel inside, the Holy Spirit will keep giving you more of your heavenly prayer language.

Pray in the Spirit (with your new prayer language) every day and talk to God often. He will be your best friend. Read your Bible regularly! Find a translation that you like and that is enjoyable for you to read. (And we recommend starting with the book of John in the New Testament.) Find a good Bible-based church that boldly preaches the Word of God and obeys what it says.

And, start to connect with other Christians as well! It will strengthen your faith and walk with God to be around other believers. God has added you into a new family; you now have new brothers and sisters in Christ! You are now part of God's family!

We would love to hear from you if you prayed this prayer today. Feel free to call or e-mail us at:

E-mail: TheTeam@whatmattersmm.org
Phone: (719) 495-9494
Web site: www.whatmattersmm.org

About the Author

Bethany and her husband Andrew are the proud parents of three wonderful children.

Bethany is the eldest daughter of Ivan and Kimberly Tait. She is an ordained minister and a leading partner of What Matters Ministries & Missions—a ministry whose heart is to rescue orphans and widows, feed the poor, build the local church, and win souls around the world.

Bethany's heart and passion are in seeing people live in the fullness of God's plan for their lives—having a close, personal relationship with Him. Her love and charisma are contagious, flowing from her own beautiful relationship with the Lord.